Managing Layoffs: 24 Tips to Downsize with Dignity

BY TRACY SHROYER, PHD

Published by Beyond the Stone Wall LLC
ISBN-13 978-1974308095

Printed in the United States of America

FIRST EDITION

Copy and Line Editing by Kim Justen, Just Write! Communications
Photo on front cover from Canva via an Extended License Agreement
Photo on back cover by Allie Acosta, Allie's Photography

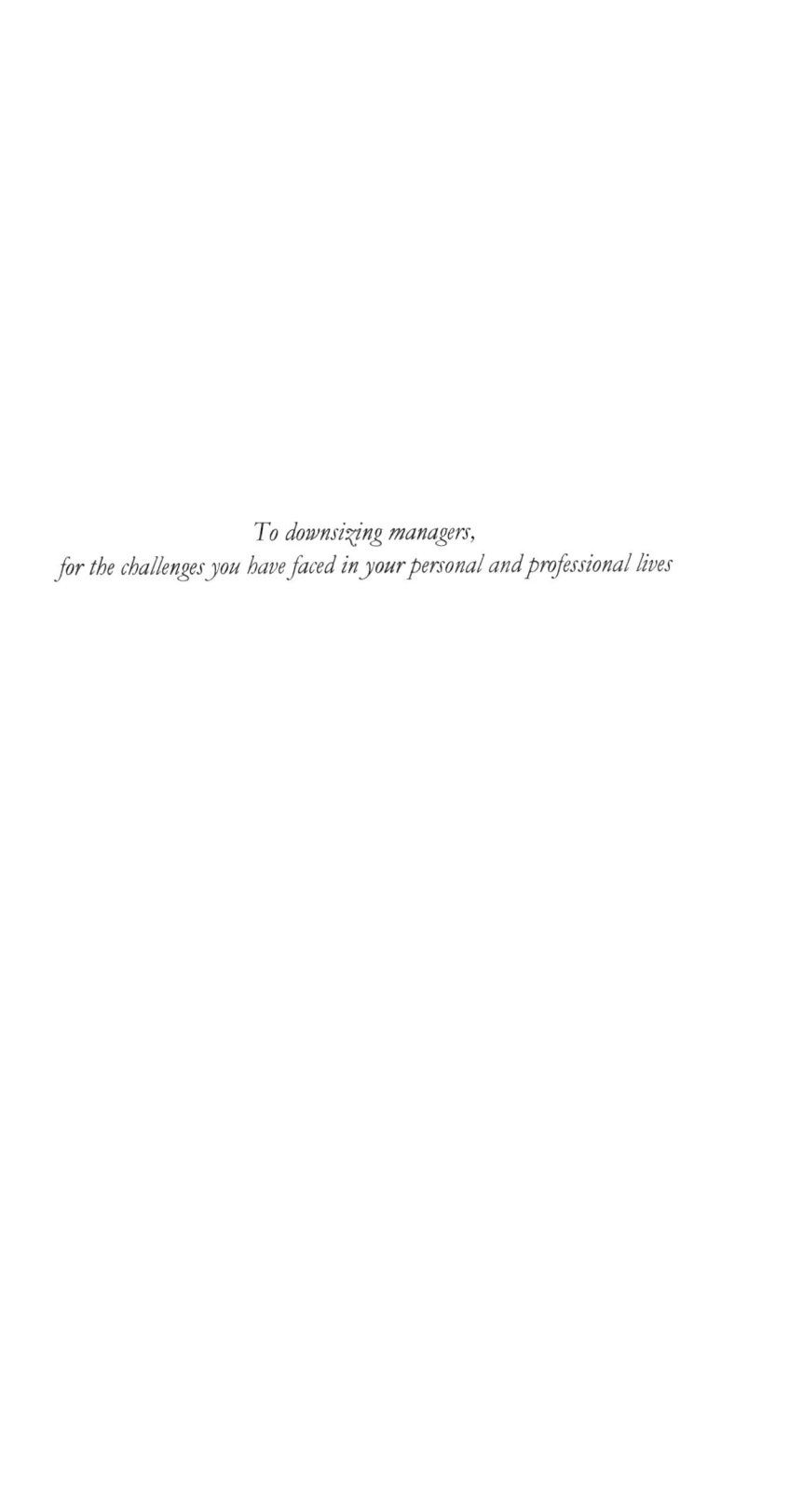

To downsizing managers,
for the challenges you have faced in your personal and professional lives

Contents

Preface

My interest in writing about managers facing the prospect of a downsizing began just over a decade ago. I remember being a survivor of downsizing within my own organization and wanted to know more about the challenges managers were facing in having to decide who goes and who stays, implement those decisions, and manage in the aftermath of those life-altering decisions. As I began to explore the topic more, I was not surprised to see the roll of eyes or heavy sighs when speaking with employees who had been laid off from, or survived a downsizing within, their organization. Having never had the experience of being a manager faced with the decision making or implementation in a layoff situation, many of these employees felt the management team was greedy and out for themselves. Heck, I even felt this way before I started to dig further into the subject.

Upon further investigation and research, what I uncovered was just the opposite. Managers who had dealt with layoffs, whether in a past or current company, mostly knew they were being trusted, and felt the heavy burden of the responsibility that came with their power. In my research, I was fortunate to interview fourteen downsizing managers, ranging from front-line managers all the way up to the Chief Executive Officers. I treated those recordings and transcripts like gold, as I knew each of their stories was important.

Through this book, I am grateful for the opportunity to bring you a thought-provoking combination of research, storytelling, and tips to downsize with dignity. There are eight total themes I will walk you through, providing you with three initial tips to downsize with dignity. I ask that you think through these tips as not only advice for when a layoff situation is imminent, but identify ways in which you can integrate these tips throughout your organization at any point in time. The more open the lines of communication are between employees and management, the better the likelihood that a smooth transition amidst change becomes possible.

Introduction

If you do not know anyone who has been impacted by layoffs, whether from the manager/employee or laid off/survivor perspective, you may be living under a rock – or better yet, you are a fortunate soul. My hope is that your organization can instead leverage alternatives to layoffs to prevent the devastating impact layoffs can cause. While there are numerous articles, blogs, books, and resources for laid off employees, the availability of such material or resources when it comes to managing layoffs from a leadership perspective are few and far between.

This book begins to fill the existing gap, and provides insight into a manager's involvement with layoffs through stories based on evidence I obtained from the experiences of past research participants. I then took my research and applied it to fictional situations to provide you with an enhanced comprehension of the provided management tips. It embraces all levels of management, from front-line managers up through the senior executive ranks, regardless of industry.

This book is a guide like no other, providing managers with tips on how to more effectively communicate regardless of whether layoffs are expected, unexpected, or not even on the horizon. To ensure we are on the same page regarding terminology, the term *layoff(s)* is defined within this book as *the elimination of existing employees' positions*, and is synonymous with the term *downsizing*. When it comes to layoffs, this book is an essential source of information for managers to have on hand and use to effectively transform into action.

The Layoff Roller Coaster

Layoffs have moved to the forefront of survival for organizations as "the quickest way to cut costs and bring about immediate, visible improvements to the bottom line" (Smith, Wright, & Huo, 2008). The increase in globalization, technological advances, deregulation, and growing domestic and foreign competition, has led to an increased use of layoffs to reduce expenses *and* achieve greater efficiency and effectiveness. In some instances, employees could see the writing on the wall due to their company's experience(s) with financial, regulatory, legal, competitive market, or other significant issues. Unfortunately, there are also many cases where employees felt they had no indication or clue layoffs were imminent.

In 1996, the United States Bureau of Labor Statistics first recorded mass layoffs – layoffs involving 50 or more employees in an organization. There is a correlation between mass layoffs and gross domestic product (GDP) as, whenever the gross domestic product decreases significantly, such as in 2001, 2008, and 2009; mass layoffs increase dramatically. Here are just a few examples of internet search result headlines related to layoffs during the timeframes noted above:

- Boeing to lay off up to 30,000, September 19, 2001, CNN.com
- Big Job Cuts at Bank of America, December 11, 2008, NYTimes.com
- Caterpillar Moves to Cut 20,000 Jobs, NYTimes.com (2009)

Although the Bureau of Labor Statistics stopped recording mass layoffs as of March 2013 (due to governmental budget cuts), news and social media platforms reveal that layoffs are on the rise again. In correlation, a dip in gross domestic product has occurred, which represents that history is likely continuing to repeat itself. Here are examples of internet search result headlines related to more recent layoffs that support this:

- Microsoft Cuts 18,000 Jobs, July 17, 2014, CNN.com
- Macy's layoffs: Over 4,000 jobs being cut, January 6, 2016, CNNMoney.com Money
- Lowes Layoffs 2017 – Worst Kept Secret in Corporate History, TheLayoff.com

With the continued use of layoffs across numerous industries, it is interesting that limited additional studies or materials have become available to support managers within those organizations to prepare for, implement, and recover from these traumatic events.

Organizational Change Studies

Organizations endure a significant amount of change based on numerous factors, including, but not limited to: globalization, technological advances, deregulation, and growing domestic and foreign competition. Organizational change can occur in one of two ways:

1. reorganizing roles and/or eliminating jobs, or
2. creating efficiencies in business processes.

Leadership teams often find it difficult to change in one aspect without blending into the other, therefore, people and processes are normally impacted.

In 1930, Kurt Lewin's Harwood Studies broke significant ground in organizational change and organizational behavior research, and helped to move his work on change from the laboratory to the office – or from theory to practice. The Harwood Studies, like many other organizational studies, such as the Hawthorne experiments, Maslow's hierarchy of needs, Herzberg's work on motivation, and McGregor's Theory X and Theory Y approach to management, provided meaningful and continually useful contributions to organizational literature.

Within the organizational change research, numerous studies related to layoffs have taken place. The primary focus of those studies has been on the impact of layoffs on employees – whether looking at downsized employees or survivors. Two studies were found that provided a focus on managers involved in layoffs. One of those studies was from Armstrong-Stassen (2005), who compared executive- and middle-level managers relative to job security and performance, use of coping skills, and health symptoms before, during, and after downsizing. The other study was conducted by Gandolfi (2009), who studied a single case of Australian bank managers' experience throughout downsizing. Both studies focused on specific factors of the managers' experiences throughout downsizing, with only one being conducted on managers within the United States. This makes it unrealistic to try to generalize any of the findings.

Despite the popularity of layoffs as a tactical means for business to stay afloat, limited literature or research focuses on the manager's experience throughout a layoff situation. This book is one step in the direction of providing a focus and guidance to managers in their time of greatest need.

Theme #1:
Communicating a Shared Vision

A company's vision defines the pathway forward, or direction, for an organization. For a company to move closer to its vision, there must be top-down communication of the vision, including the purpose and the anticipated impact, or result, once achieved. Without this communication throughout the organization, employees may feel lost and unsure of what leadership wants to achieve. Understanding and acceptance of the vision is another reason to ensure employees receive this communication. Employee support will provide needed support to help drive the company towards its defined vision.

Communication is a critical tool in initiating and managing change. Supporting organizational change results either in a need to move closer to the company's existing vision, or the realization of the need to transition towards a new vision. Without communication, the change will be extremely challenging and more likely to fail. There are many platforms managers have in which to communicate with their employees, such as holding meetings with individuals or teams, management by walking around and talking to employees regularly, or in appropriate social settings (e.g., lunch, employer reunions). Managers should use these communication techniques year-round, and not only when change is in sight. Employees will catch on and realize the false intent if these techniques are not used genuinely. It is important for management to understand the importance of maintaining open and honest communication with employees, as it builds credibility and trust – elements critical in dealing with change.

Adam's Story

After more than 20 years in an organization within the communications industry, Adam faced his most significant experience as a manager. He was called into his manager's office and told the devastating news: layoffs were imminent and it was going to be a significant hit to his department – over 40% would be downsized. Over the next few months, Adam attended numerous meetings with Human Resources to determine all the logistics, including who would go, how employee discussions would occur, what types of severance packages would be available, and how the remaining department employees would manage the most critical processes. This took a significant amount of time and commitment to those involved in the decision making, implementation, and department management in the aftermath of the layoffs.

Although Adam had experienced layoffs as a manager before, it was for a much smaller company and the process was handled much differently. During the current instance, his manager kept him and his peer at arms-length – often it seemed that Adam's manager was hiding behind his office door, not wanting to face the reality of the situation. Adam linked his manager's current behavior to the same stoic behavior when any type of conflict had arisen in the past, and considered it a sign of weakness in the person who was supposed to be more of a role model for him and other managers in the organization. Despite his manager's demeanor, Adam saw his role as an extremely valuable experience in that he was recognized for understanding the big picture of the company. He realized that he was charged with an awesome responsibility to help build the future, while at the same time being recognized as having the compassion and the ability to be able to deliver the message in a way that would be received in an optimal way to where the individual would not feel persecuted.

Adam accepted the news that the layoffs were going to happen. His initial reaction was the feeling of being punched in the gut, and he was taken back to his prior experience as a downsizing manager. Once those feelings began to subside and the reality of the situation hit, he knew he was in the position where it was important to communicate the direction of the organization, and the impacts on its employees and their processes. Adam's ability and history in openly communicating with his direct reports and their employees is one reason that this experience would run as smoothly as possible. Adam's tone was serious yet compassionate when he addressed his staff, and he talked to them about how the downsizing process would work. What no one realized was that, after the last manager left and Adam's office door closed, he looked at the picture of his own family on his desk and he wept.

The plan Adam shared with his management team was that they would first need to bring their department's employees together within the next week. During that meeting, Adam let everyone know that, despite the attempts over the last year to cut expenses using authorized unpaid days off, cancelling the company's annual conference, and 5% salary reductions across the organization, the executive leadership team confirmed staff cuts were now unavoidable.

Most of Adam's employees had 12 or more years of tenure, and many had stayed in the same department their entire time with the company. The news came as a shock to some, but not many, as Adam had been open with them over the last year, when it came to the need to implement the other cost-cutting strategies. He was sure to let his employees know that, although it would likely cause some challenges in their processes, these were methods the organization was using to minimize expenses and hopefully avoid any more significant and life-altering impact to its personnel. Adam was frustrated with himself for not realizing earlier that he couldn't be more wrong when he said those things to his team.

Adam had always been an open book, and numerous employees referenced his ability to do this well, while not overstepping the confidential nature of the projects and personnel issues. The executive team and his peers across the organization saw him as someone in the ideal position due to his vast skill set, which included his ability to recommend alternatives when the decision on the table was highly impactful to employees or customers. Over the years, he built trust from the front-line up because of his openness and willingness to be authentic and honest. Employees had grown to trust Adam and understood that he did what he could to minimize impacts to his people and their processes. There were several managers in the organization, including Adam's own, who did not bear these qualities – some did not even come close.

What Adam said and did, as well as what he didn't say and do, were a reflection on him and the management team. Timely and concise communication up, down, and across the organization, reduces negative effects, as it provides clarity and greater understanding. Open and honest communication by managers within the organization increases the likelihood of employees' openness and motivation to change. Adam's team knew he would do what he could to support them during a difficult time, whether that meant setting aside time to talk about their fears, scheduling resources to come in for career support for employees being downsized, or providing regular updates to increase awareness and decrease anxiety, to the greatest extent possible.

After the initial announcement about the layoffs, a small group of survivors got together to voice their concerns with Adam. Their fear was regarding the workload and stress they all felt would ensue after the downsized employees' last day. Adam listened to them attentively and talked with them about the opportunity for them to become even more empowered than they had been in the past. He met with them a little over a week later, walking into the conference room with a small bag. The bag contained about a dozen colorful sticky note pads. Adam dumped them onto the table and asked each person to grab one.

Then he proceeded to walk them through an exercise to talk about the current processes within the department, and who was responsible for which process. Two hours later, the group wrapped up their meeting and felt a little less anxious. The butterflies in their stomachs were still there, but they were getting calmer because of the work they had just done. This wasn't the end of the exercise though. They still had quite a bit of work left to do before they felt things were going to be okay – maybe not perfect, but enough for them to handle the current situation and not feel the stress and burnout employees in other departments were likely to experience.

On the last day of work for the 26 downsized employees in his department, Adam left his house without eating breakfast and barely sipping from his coffee. His stomach was in knots, despite the last few weeks and months going by with little issue. He knew the ins and outs of the next steps for many of his employees, as he made sure to maintain updates and keep his door open to working through the change with them since it was first announced.

Three employees found work right after the announcement and left immediately without notice, too hurt to say much to anyone. Four employees refused the career search help provided and were doing the bare minimum until their time was up. Adam ached for not being able to help those individuals more and it pained him to think they might think poorly of the organization or him. Eight employees decided retirement was the best option for them, while the remaining 11 met frequently with the career search resources brought in and had new positions at local organizations lined up for the coming weeks. As he was driving to the office that day, a smile crossed his face thinking of those employees he could support – including those employees that were not laid off: the *survivors*.

Reflection Questions

1. *Which of Adam's actions would you have a difficult time implementing? Why?*

2. *If Adam could hold an hour-long meeting with his peers after the initial announcement of layoffs to employees, what two topics would you recommend he discuss with them?*

3. *What do you think the small, concerned group of employees who met with Adam did next?*

"One of the toughest challenges facing organizations [amidst change] today is to generate employee commitment to vision and business strategy." – Shaffer[1]

Tips & Best Practices for Communicating a Shared Vision

1. <u>Develop a well-planned vision that is easy to understand</u>

Through a vision, an organization answers the question: "What do we want to achieve?" in a unique and simplistic statement. How does an organization know what to do if it doesn't know where it wants to go?

The vision provides purpose and incorporates the organization's values.

One of Stephen Covey's 7 Habits is "keep the end in mind," as it is essential to lay out a clear vision. A clear vision provides employees with a focal point of reference, ensuring processes and behaviors consistently relate back to the vision. Take the following into consideration when developing or re-evaluating your organization's vision:

- What does the organization want to achieve?
- What is the new expectation or the organization's newly planned future state?
- What does the organization want to provide (to its clients/customers, partners, employees, etc.)?

To ensure employees support the company's vision, the language and content should be clear, simple, and inspiring.

2.   Communicate the reason change is needed

Regardless of how many products/services, processes, or people are impacted by change within the organization, it is critical to ensure open communication as to the reason for the changes. Change within a company can occur for any number of reasons. Maybe the company needs to become more competitive in the marketplace to stay afloat in the industry. Therefore, there is a strong need to integrate and launch more innovative products and services. If one area does not obtain approval to replace headcount due to attrition, because of a need to put that headcount elsewhere in the organization, there should be honesty around that. The truth might sting initially, but it has a way of building trust in leadership. Keeping the reasons for change under wraps will only allow the rumor mill to run wild.

Even if the whole truth cannot be shared, possibly due to legal, financial, or other concerns, managers owe their employees the respect of not being completely ambiguous. Rather, what *can* the manager say regarding the reason for change. Maybe it is a result of timing, and the manager can only share the reason after a certain date. If that is the case – keep that promise and don't continue to lead employees down a path thinking they will find out by a set date and end up disappointed once that date occurs.

Ensure that as a manager, thought leadership goes into the right thing to say to employees when change is needed.

3.   <u>Provide consistent messaging – you cannot overcommunicate</u>

Not only should employees be communicated with in an open and honest manner, but that communication also needs to be timely and consistent. Sharing information after the fact – especially much later – plays a part in breaking down trust between employees and managers. Tell them. Tell them you told them. Tell them again. This ensures they receive the message. I have realized this is true with any group. With all the information that is communicated, it can be difficult to keep track of everything. Guaranteeing your message gets heard is important.

Theme #2:
Managing Resistance to Change

Greek philosopher, Heraclitus, said, "The only thing constant is change." There should be no surprise when a manager encounters employees, peers, or even senior leaders in the organization who react to change with shock and fear. One thing that has not changed enough over time is people's ability to deal with change – whether that means being proactive and responding with action versus mind-numbing surprise. There are several ways to ensure individuals across the organization are more prepared for change; they help minimize the impact and potential resistance when it appears.

Carly's Story

She barely made it to her car before the tears came too quickly for one tissue to absorb. An unplanned end of day meeting had just ended 10 minutes earlier in which Carly and her peers found out that their company, Cooper's, a popular department store in the Midwest and Eastern United States, was going to be acquired by Retail City, an even more popular one-stop-shop retail store out West. Although Carly had only been a VP at Cooper's for the last two years, she felt like she was part of the family their culture instilled. An almost 50-year-old family business, and during her first few days with the organization, she instantly knew this was the place for her. She felt like she fit in, was respected, and cared for by her manager, peers, and the employees.

Carly knew the next few weeks were going to be the hardest to overcome. She had to first figure out how to accept the reality of the acquisition and try to calm the fears of what that might mean. When she got to work the next morning, she closed her office door, took out a fresh notepad and wrote down the following: *Reasons Why this Change Might be a Good Thing.* Underneath, she began the list with:

Increase awareness of both brands across the U.S.

Tapping her pen to her forehead, she then proceeded to add:

Potential job growth or change

At that moment, her face crinkled up and she couldn't stop the thought of just the opposite: potential job loss. "What if…," she thought, then quickly opened her desk drawer and dropped the notepad in and slammed the drawer shut. She jumped out of her chair, deciding a nice cup of coffee might help decrease the devil's advocate from stomping all over her list of reasons why the acquisition might just be a good thing.

During the prior Friday meeting, Carly's boss, Mike, told her and her peers that within one week the announcement of the acquisition would be public. All the employees at Cooper's and Retail City would find out only a couple hours before the press release was sent and the world knew. Between now and then, the hard work would be starting to figure out what the acquisition meant and how the management team might be able to calm employees' fears, and help them to see the potential in this change. Carly knew she had to figure out more items to add to the list she had started if she was going to be even half convincing to anyone else when news release day came.

The next day, Carly was meeting with one of her peers, Gwen, in her office. They started to talk about the news and Gwen was filled with excitement over the possibilities this held for both companies. Carly pulled out her notepad and told Gwen about the list she was trying to build, in part because she herself was skeptical about what good may come from this huge change.

Gwen proceeded to share an experience from 3 years before, when she was a VP of Operations at another retailer and they decided to merge with a smaller retailer to increase their product selection. As expected, Gwen shared there had been anxiety and worry on behalf of both companies' employees, but everything turned out for the best. Fears were alleviated when employees at both companies were evaluated for their strengths and it was determined that some functions needed centralization, such as Human Resources and Sales. This didn't necessarily mean a cut to staff in these areas though.

As the HR and Training teams identified the strengths among all employees within these groups, they realized the need for those strengths in other areas for the new combined company to realize results. Yes, some employees were not happy with the process or changes and decided to leave the company, but that was helpful in that no one else needed to be let go.

Carly looked down at her list when Gwen took a breath, and decided to add two more reasons to her list:

Use of employees' strengths across existing or (possibly) new teams
Natural attrition for those uncomfortable with the change

Later that afternoon, with the notepad still on her desk, Carly thought of one more to add:

Different cultures merging – possible to take best of both worlds?

She now had a total of five items on her Reasons Why this Change Might be a Good Thing list:

Increase awareness of both brands across the U.S.
Potential job growth or change
Use of employees' strengths across existing or (possibly) new teams
Natural attrition for those uncomfortable with the change
Different cultures merging – possible to take best of both worlds?

It was well past 6 p.m. and Carly knew her husband would be waiting for her to arrive for dinner in the next half hour. Once again, she opened her desk drawer and placed the notepad in it. This time, as she did so, she was beginning to think this whole acquisition might not be as bad as she initially thought.

Thankfully, Carly was right. The acquisition happened and, although there were a few bumps along the way, the outcome was overall positive for the organization and its employees.

There were employees that were ready for retirement and had the chance to take advantage of it, and others that could move into another area of the company based on their skill sets and the company's needs.

Reflection Questions

1. *Why do you think Carly decided to create her Reasons Why this Change Might be a Good Thing list? Would this approach have helped you if you were in a situation like hers?*

2. *Gwen talked about her prior experience and how it turned out to be something beneficial to the companies that merged. What similarities and differences are there between Gwen's prior experience and what Cooper's and Retail City are getting ready to go through? How could that impact the outcome?*

3. *How could Carly's leadership team have further involved her ahead of time so that the change was not what felt like a sudden change to her?*

"It is not the strongest of the species that survives, nor the most intelligent that survives. It is the one that is the most adaptable to change." – Charles Darwin

Tips & Best Practices for Managing Resistance to Change

1. <u>Set the expectation that change is inevitable – it matters most how we react</u>

To help minimize the resistance to change, it is healthy for managers to ensure their team members know change is constant and the only way to have any control over it is to be prepared and ready to act. Employees' awareness of their role in the organization, the state of the industry and economy, and the organization's importance and impact overall, are potential indicators of what may happen. Long gone are the days of working for an organization for 20+ years.

Employees must open themselves up to new opportunities and learn how to be somewhat comfortable with ambiguity. In a world of never-ending change, it is so important to advocate for oneself and take control where possible.

2.   Involve employees in the change

Communicating with employees prior to, during, and after the change will decrease the likelihood of employee resistance as management has worked to build a level of trust and understanding. This is not to say there will not be any resistance, but these types of steps and involvement have been known to help minimize shock and fear, and allow the change to occur a bit smoother than otherwise possible.

Adam's story from the previous chapter provides a better example of being able to openly communicate with employees and ensure they had awareness of what was being done and considered throughout the process, as well as what the future impact would be based on the results of those actions. In this chapter's story, Carly was in a tough spot, as employees were not allowed to be made aware until a few hours prior to the press release. What may have been the result if employees were aware of the acquisition much earlier in the process? Is there any way Carly could have talked with her manager about being able to make this happen?

3.   Think about resistance to change from downsized employees, surviving employees, and other managers' perspectives

As a manager, put yourself in your employees' shoes – whether they have been identified both as someone who will be let go and will stay. Think about the worries and challenges each will face, and consider the opportunities that appear because of their fate. One participant in my dissertation noted this, related to a downsized employee perspective:

> How do you know that this one person wasn't sitting at a barbeque with his best friend on Saturday and said, "You know, if I ever got laid off, I'd flip the freaking table over or I'd piss on their desk." You know, how do you know that it doesn't happen? You can just

never take anything for granted and I don't try to ever ask why they acted that way. You just accept it. Honestly, I don't know what I would do. People cry, get emotional, [and] walk out. I could be one of those people that just get up and leave.

Think also through the lens of an employee who survived a downsizing. There could be *feelings of relief* that they still have a position and will not have to experience a significant life change; *feelings of anger*, in that their friends or family were let go, or due to the amount of work that may be left to handle; or more likely, *a mixture of both relief, anger, fear, and numerous other emotions.*

After looking at the roles from different perspectives, think about what opportunities a manager has in preparing employees for potential changes, including improving communication. What more could a manager learn from their employees prior to, during, or after, an organizational change? How could that alter the way managers interact when there is no sign of change on the line?

Theme #3:
Securing Commitment and Loyalty

Prior to any type of change occurring in an organization, the management team must look for ways in which to secure commitment and loyalty from employees. Employee commitment can be comprised of: a belief in the organization's vision; passion and support of the products or services being offered; agreement of the way the organization does business; and the perspective that a strong leadership team exists. Let's break this down a bit more.

Are *employees aware of the organization's vision*, and is it a strong enough vision to carry the company into the future against things like globalization, technological advances, deregulation, and growing domestic and foreign competition? If not, what should be revamped within the vision, mission, and goals to align appropriately to the future possibilities? Don't become the next Kodak, or Blockbuster Video. Those companies were not willing to adjust to the times. Think about it – if there was appropriate innovation within Blockbuster's site, could they have come up with the Netflix concept?

Are the *organization's employees passionate and supportive of the products or services offered?* Are employees within the company's target market – if so, are they purchasing the company's products or services over competitors? If not, that is a problem. Their commitment to the company is only as much as the paycheck coming in every two weeks or the next best offer that may come along.

Do *employees understand how the company operates* – whether it is the team they are part of, or thinking about the bigger picture? Is there an opportunity for efficiency in the processes that currently exist? The level of employee commitment will rise if there is a stake in the way business is done, whether by allowing them to help identify efficiencies through innovation programs, or asking an employee to identify an opportunity for improvement and allowing them to take the lead.

How do *employees treat the leadership team* within the organization? Does there appear to be a level of respect or a change in demeanor (i.e., whispers, eye rolling, sighs) when a member of leadership is mentioned? Employees who know the members of the company's leadership team – even if it is just name or facial recognition – are more likely to be committed to the success of the organization.

There are several ways to identify the commitment and loyalty that employees may have to their organization. A few questions to identify employees' level of commitment and loyalty include:

1. Do employees understand the company's vision?
2. Are they passionate supportive of the products or services offered?
3. Do they understand how the company operates?
4. How do employees treat the leadership team?

Nina's Story

Nina rubbed her growing pregnant belly, only thinking all the while about the families who were going to be impacted by the news of the upcoming downsizing. She was thankful she was not among the list of those being let go, but she realized that could change at any time. Unfortunately, or possibly fortunately, Nina's strength was in planning and implementing layoffs in a smooth fashion. She had done so well at it that she was highly sought after in the financial services industry. Last month marked Nina's five-year anniversary with Abacus Financial Services in Chicago. She was now just over six months pregnant with her first child and was finding it more difficult to hold back the emotions that this role and her pregnancy hormones were creating lately.

This was the first organization that Nina had been at for more than four years, and while there were challenges the organization was facing lately, she was committed to seeing her role through, or to the extent through that they would allow her. Her smooth, but direct tone, as well as her ability to maintain reason and fairness, proved extremely beneficial in laying a solid foundation for the first of three phases of layoffs, all which would occur within the next two months.

Recently, a friend of Nina's asked if she felt loyal to her current organization. With a few moments of silence, she took a deep breath and said that she had some degree of loyalty in the role and responsibilities she held in return for being able to receive the paycheck the organization provided her every week. She continued by stating she felt her loyalty was to the people she had to displace through the layoffs.

Early in the process of assessing work teams and employees prior to identifying who would go and who would stay with this reorganization, Nina worked with each manager to gather performance indicators as well as background on the employees – such as any issues within their employee files, awards received, committee contributions, innovations approved, etc. During part of that process, a few managers also mentioned (without Nina's asking, and not part of the process) the level of commitment they felt certain employees had to the organization.

When it came time to deliver the news to the employees being let go, Nina was not surprised at the reactions she received from a few people, as she had seen that behavior in the past. What did surprise her was that two of the employees being downsized (from two different teams) had been noted as having a low commitment to the company, and they reacted so negatively to the news that the police were called to escort them off the property that day. Nina only knew of the commitment levels for some of the employees that were being let go, and one aspect she noticed for this reorganization was that the employees who were noted as being highly committed to the organization were clearly upset at the news, but took it better than those she had been told were less loyal.

Reflection Questions

1. *How much impact do you believe the level of commitment and loyalty really played in the reactions of the employees Nina had to downsize?*

2. *Do you believe loyalty and commitment plays a significant role in the reactions of downsized employees overall?*

3. *Nina responded to her friend that her loyalty was to the employees she was having to let go, and ensuring a smooth transition in that process. What are some of the steps she was likely to take to ensure this happened?*

"Unless commitment is made, there are only promises and hopes; but no plans."
— Peter F. Drucker

Tips & Best Practices for Securing Commitment and Loyalty

1. Build relationships with others in the organization.

There is a significant opportunity lost by managers who choose to stay along in their office rather than open the door and invite others in, or leave the space and talk with employees. Getting to know employees and being there for them allows a manager to build relationships. The interactions must be genuine if a manager wants employees to feel they can be open and let the manager know what they are working on, what concerns they have, and maybe even a little about them personally (what are their areas of passion, hobbies, etc.). I have several managers to this day who I keep in touch with and may reach out to for insight or feedback. Those managers were the ones who knew building our relationship was important to my commitment to the work, to them, and to the organization.

2. Speak the truth and align behaviors, attitudes, and words.

An effective manager is a role model to others in the organization as to how to behave, act, and communicate. Managers with these abilities who are willing to help employees improve upon these types of skills have a way of increasing the commitment employees have in them. Managers who speak the truth and align behaviors, attitudes, and words build credibility and make employees want to follow them and do their best.

3. Let go. If employees are not willing to commit and want to leave, let them.

A manager can only try to hold on to an employee so much.

People are entitled to make their own decisions in what they feel is in their best interest. Managers can only provide them with the information they have available and ask employees for their commitment. If that is not enough, it is not enough, and the manager has no control over employees' reactions.

Theme #4:
Maintaining or Restoring
Morale and Motivation

Change is stressful, regardless of whether the change is positive or negative. Organizational change typically leads to decreased morale and motivation prior to, during, and after the change. There may be fear, anxiety, nervousness, excitement – a whole range of emotions are possible during times like these. Employees may appear perfectly fine one day, and then have extremely low morale the next day. It is difficult for most employees to remove the personal impact and resulting feelings from the workplace in times of change. If not monitored by individuals, their source of support, or surviving leadership; these emotions may escalate and result in further individual or organizational issues.

Effective managers pay attention to the level of morale and motivation within the organizational overall, within their team, as well as their own personal motivation. By evaluating the level of morale and motivation in the organization, team, and self, a manager can then identify what actions need to occur to help restore or maintain it. Communication is critical throughout change, including the need for managers to ensure they are aware of what types of actions and words impact employees' morale and motivation levels.

Priyanka's Story

It had been a full two weeks now since the downsizing occurred and thirty-four people (out of 224 total employees) officially left the organization. Priyanka was doing her best to move on, and she realized her ability to hold things together was a saving grace to the surviving employees on her team. The challenge was that the downsizing felt like it came out of nowhere, and within a week of the announcement, laid off employees were handing in their badges and walking out the door one last time.

Priyanka had only been a manager for eight months, and was still getting the hang of how the world of management in an Operations environment worked. She was extremely thankful to have a strong mentor in Mike, the Department Manager in Marketing. He helped her through the last couple months when the organization's most difficult times were upon them. Mike had experienced downsizing before with two other organizations in his career and gave Priyanka advice that really helped her build trust with her employees and begin to build a foundation for the post-downsizing environment in the months ahead.

Through the downsizing, Priyanka lost a total of two of her then eleven-person team. With the remaining nine employees, she was most challenged with increasing morale and motivation. They were performing at the minimum standards, which she was thankful for. She was well-aware not all teams were keeping up at this point. Her concern was that it wouldn't take much for a slump to occur and picking up from the current state would be a whole lot easier than waiting for something to happen.

She had a meeting scheduled with Mike for the next afternoon and she decided to write a few thoughts down so she wouldn't forget.

How can I work with my team to improve our results?
What will help to motivate my team?

When it came time for Priyanka's meeting with Mike, she was glad that she had written down her thoughts the day before. She'd had so much going through her head since the day the change was announced that she was fearful she would have completely forgotten what her thoughts were.

She shared her thoughts with Mike and asked him what ideas he had. Thankfully, Mike had read two books in the last year that really spoke to Priyanka's questions: *Start with Why* by Simon Sinek, and *The Truth about Employee Engagement* by Patrick Lencioni. He recommended first that Priyanka read these, and promised to bring his copies in for her.

After reading both books, Priyanka felt like she had an epiphany. She personally knew her own *why*, but she didn't know enough about her team or their *why*. In the past, it was a challenge to find time, primarily due to her own schedule, to have one-on-one meetings with each of her employee's other than once a month. She knew this had to change for her to increase her ability to motivate her employees. So many ideas began to fill her head, so she quickly grabbed a couple sheets of paper and wrote down her thoughts, which included:

- *Change team meeting frequency from 2-hours once a month to 30-minutes per week*
- *Change employee one-on-ones from once a month to twice a month*
- *Team doesn't realize value of their work, despite completing month-end reports*
  - *Identify how to involve them more in that process, have discussions about what is reported; and*
  - *Get their input on if the items being reported really reflect their work and value – if not, figure out how to integrate those pieces*
- *Figure out opportunity for teambuilding – maybe once every 6 months?*

If she wanted to keep the lines of communication open with her employees and have any chance of improving morale, she knew these changes were critical. To be motivated to improve, Priyanka felt the team also needed to realize what the results meant to the organization and the impact her team made overall.

Reflection Questions

1. *Do you think the changes Priyanka identified will increase morale within her team?*

2. *What other opportunities might Priyanka have to motivate her team?*

3. *How might Priyanka's own _why_, as well as the _why_ of her team members, play a*

   role amidst the change?

"I think a lot of times it's not money that is the primary motivation factor; it's the passion for your job and the professional and personal satisfaction that you get out of doing what you do that motivates you." – Martin Yan, Chinese Chef

Tips & Best Practices for Maintaining or Restoring Morale and Motivation

1. <u>Be present.</u>

There is nothing worse than an employee unable to access their own manager for guidance or feedback. It is important for a manager to be present and available to employees as often as possible. This is not only in relation to being available (whether that means being in the office, available via e-mail or on instant messenger), it also means the manager is mentally *there* and engaged with the employee. The latter part of this may be challenging due to the number of potential distractions surrounding managers. A couple methods to avoid those distractors *when focusing on the needs of an employee* are to mark yourself as 'Do Not Disturb' on phone and instant messenger, or consider going to a different place physically, to provide for an atmosphere where the focus can be directed to the employee. Giving this focus to an employee builds trust.

2. <u>Be aware.</u>

It is always beneficial for a manager to know his or her employees. It could be knowing who they are, what they do, where they struggle, or what they want to achieve professionally. Unfortunately, there are managers that do not take the time to get to know their employees. When that happens and another opportunity pops up, it may be an easy choice for the employee to walk away from the team. Teams with managers who care about them and show interest, build trust and respect more easily.

3. <u>Identify employees' motivators.</u>

Employees are typically motivated by several factors at work. These may be intrinsic, extrinsic, or a mix of both. Examples of intrinsic motivators include someone feeling like they are doing a good job, or being given the ability to take on more responsibility. Examples of extrinsic motivators are the tangible take-aways, such as the paycheck, bonus, prizes, an appreciation meal, and more. When it comes to employee motivators there is no "one size fits all" – despite money being a significant motivator. As a manager, it is important to understand the unique motivators specific to each person on the team. This can be done through a discussion with employees during their one-on-ones, or through a survey via paper or e-mail. Knowing what motivates team members is only part of the equation, using those motivators at appropriate times and frequencies is the other crucial piece.

Theme #5:
Maintaining Productivity
or Job Performance

Although there is a positive correlation between training and development and organizational performance,[1] senior leadership within organizations often translate the time and resource needs for training and development not worth the monetary and opportunity cost. As a result, a manager's ability to adequately manage employee issues throughout the layoff experience typically proves to be a challenge.

From the first potential word of layoffs, all the way through an actual layoff experience, employees may show an increase, decrease, or mix of productivity. News and social media may have a negative impact on performance; whereas employees worrying about whether they will still have a job may reflect more positive performance results to ensure their value is reflected within the organization. After multiple rounds of layoffs, there is likely to be a decrease in productivity, as the willingness to work and expected survival diminishes with each announcement.

Emily's Story

Emily, the Warehouse Director at MacInrow's Shipping, had been with the company for over a decade and her intuition had always served her well. With the company's recent layoffs, Emily knew that many of the employees in her department were struggling. She did not realize the severity of impact that the changes were having on Charlotte, one of her direct reports. It would not take long for Emily to begin realizing that Charlotte's reaction to the layoffs was negatively impacting her team.

Jason never thought he would be considered one of them – a *survivor*. Through all the challenges the organization he worked for had faced over the last year, he wasn't quite sure how to feel about being a survivor. In a way, he compared the downsizing at MacInrow's Shipping to a tornado, since over half of the workforce was let go. The office was barren and those remaining were walking around like zombies, not knowing quite how to react to it all.

Only the week before, totally out of the blue, members of the senior executive team at MacInrow began tapping employees on the shoulder, taking them into a private conference room, and letting them know their fates. After the layoffs, Jason's manager, Charlotte, changed for the worse. While Charlotte had not always been the best manager, she was okay. After the layoffs, she became a manager who made her remaining employees despise Mondays, Tuesdays, and all the other days of the week. She was so upset at how the layoffs were handled that she had shut herself off from feeling anything.

Without available resources (the company decided to eliminate the Employee Assistance Program to save on expenses), Charlotte continued to fall deeper and deeper into a depression. This meant that her prior focus on her role as a manager became less existent every day thereafter. Her employees were hurting too, but she didn't realize getting help for herself might be a step in helping them.

After the layoffs, the workload began to feel like it was going to be never ending as it quickly began to pile up on Jason's desk and in his e-mail. The layoffs wiped out four of his six-member team, leaving Jason and one other team member. His remaining co-worker was feeling the same struggle, and neither felt like they had a manager to support them any longer.

It was about two weeks after the layoffs that Emily began noticing Charlotte's continued absenteeism, and when she was in the warehouse it seemed as if it was only for short bouts of time and was not cognizant to the needs of her team. Charlotte's two remaining employees seemed overwhelmed and Emily knew it was important to get involved soon or she may lose Charlotte and her two remaining team members. After the layoffs, MacInrow's Shipping could not afford to lose any more employees.

Emily decided to meet with Jason and his co-worker separately to talk about the workload. While Emily couldn't change the amount of work coming in, she knew there were opportunities for efficiency in the process – which she pointed out was one of the main reasons Charlotte's team was cut so deep. It was a matter of figuring out how to make time to identify and implement those efficiencies.

Emily met again with Jason and his co-worker a week later to let them know Charlotte was no longer with the company, and their new manager was not identified yet. In the meantime, both would report to Emily. She set up two meetings per week with them to begin identifying efficiencies and developing a plan of how they could implement the most realistic opportunities.

With this change, and the increased focus Emily gave Jason and his co-worker, his job performance began to improve and he realized he wasn't as anxious as he had been about coming to work. Over the next two months, Emily, Jason, and his co-worker identified a few ideas to improve their work processes, and how to best implement two of the opportunities immediately, and re-visit another later. It wasn't easy by any means, but Emily knew the changes were necessary if Jason and his co-worker were to increase productivity and attempt to avoid burnout. She knew she had to roll up her sleeves and contribute, mainly in the preparation and implementation of the agreed upon efficiencies, since relying on two people that were already buried in business as usual processes and trying to help with this was a big ask. She knew it was a short-term need and the anticipated benefits would be Jason and his co-worker getting back to regular work hours, not feeling guilty for taking a vacation or sick day, and being productive and happy employees once again. These benefits far outweighed the cost of added work for herself in the short-term, and went far to building a relationship of trust and respect between her and her employees.

Reflection Questions

1.   *What do you think Emily might have said to Jason and his co-worker to help ease their anxiety about coming to work after the layoffs?*

2. *What types of benefits might your Employee Assistance Plan have been able to provide to any of the individuals in Emily's story?*

3. *As a manager, how could you assist if there was a deep cut or change within your current team? In what ways could you roll up your sleeves and contribute, if needed?*

"The simple act of paying positive attention to people has a great deal to do with productivity." - Tom Peters

Tips & Best Practices for Maintaining Productivity or Job Performance

1. <u>Identify a strategy to "do more with less."</u>

Emily mentioned to Jason and his co-worker that a reason for the deep cuts to their team was due to the realization that efficiencies were possible. It is utterly amazing how much waste occurs within organizations – at all levels. Think about it from this perspective – if a manager's team works four different functions and senior leadership advised that one full-time employee would need to be transitioned to another department, or laid off, how could those four functions be looked at from a different perspective? Are all four functions necessary? What steps within each of the functions could be automated, outsourced, etc.? In the story, Emily, Jason, and his co-worker identified three processes where efficiencies could be created, but realized they would have to take a phased approach. In building a plan for doing more with less, it is important to consider using a similar phased approach.

2. <u>Know the skills, strengths, knowledge, and interest of employees on your team.</u>

When change happens, there may be occasions where management grabs the first person in sight to help with a process. The better approach is for management to understand the skills, strengths, knowledge, and interests of employees on the team. Therefore, the next time something comes up, management has a better grasp on who the best person is to assist. When management grabs the first person in sight, it may take longer to execute on what is needed if the skill set does not exist for that employee, whereas an employee who is well-versed in the skill, topic, etc., and has bandwidth (or the manager can help to create bandwidth for the employee) will enable the team to see results much sooner. One way to do this is to conduct a skills, knowledge, and interest inventory with each direct report (Appendix C).

3. <u>Involve others in the planning and implementation of work efficiencies.</u>

One of the best ways to obtain employee support, especially during times of change, is to involve the employees in the planning and implementation process. This is a form of empowerment demonstrating to employees that they are valued within the organization, and reflecting that their actions or feedback can make a difference. Finding ways to empower employees before, during, or after an organizational change can prove challenging, but is invaluable in the return on the investment for leadership. This may be a matter of holding focus groups, allowing an employee or set of employees to lead a certain process change, or possibly having an innovation program that rewards employees for approved suggestions. Remember those intangible type of awards in the event the organization does not have a budget to set aside for this – such as an extra break or vacation day (if business needs allow), or public recognition at a meeting or in a newsletter.

Theme #6:
Coping with Survivor Syndrome

Survivor syndrome is a concept representative of the feelings of guilt and anxiety individuals experience after others in their organization are laid off. After layoffs, employees may experience *survivor syndrome* along with a gamut of emotions due to immense feelings of loss and being overwhelmed (as they are the ones that often pick up work left by laid off employees).

In the post-layoff environment, surviving employees may also become more introspective as to their future *with* the organization, or as to the future *of* the organization. Survivors may begin to question their role, or the value they bring to the organization. Employees may also begin to question the reason for the organizational change and what strength and sustenance the organization has within the industry.

Barbara's Story

Barbara's operational support team at Sunrise Cable was hit hard by the layoffs – in one day they lost four out of nine teammates. Everyone was feeling the loss as many of Sunrise Cable's employees were well-tenured and had grown to know and appreciate each other both in and outside of the office. Thankfully, Barbara's senior leadership team provided training for managing in the aftermath of the layoffs, including access to resources like the Employee Assistance Plan, which employees could access completely anonymously.

Barbara was engaging with every member of her team each day. Despite it being almost six weeks since that terrible day, Amber, one of the surviving members of Barbara's team, still could not seem to shake the sadness of losing some of her dearest friends, nor could she handle the guilt that was beginning to build up inside. Barbara admits she was lenient about Amber's less than successful results in the first couple of weeks after the layoffs, but began to realize if Amber wanted to stay employed, she was going to need to pull herself out of this funk.

Prior, during, and after the layoffs, the company's senior leadership team was extremely open and available, which is not always the case. Barbara was thankful for this, especially since this was her first experience as a manager amidst layoffs. She was a surviving employee of her last organization's layoffs over six years ago, and ended up leaving within a year after. The culture at that organization continued to deteriorate after the layoffs, management was even more closed off than before, and no one seemed to care whether results were achieved or not. It was a challenging environment prior to the layoffs, but that event ensured any chance of recovery was highly unlikely. Looking back, Barbara realized she made the right move in leaving, as it propelled her into a great company like Sunrise Cable, and she eventually earned her way into a management position there.

Barbara's prior experience reminded her that good can come from a life-changing event like being a layoff survivor. She needed to find a way to relay this to Amber, and see what could be done to turn around the situation for the better – for both the organization and for Amber. Each manager at Sunrise Cable was assigned to a restructuring business partner in Human Resources, and in Barbara's case that was Ivan. Ivan knew the rules, but had a considerate and caring demeanor, which was a refreshing mix given the situation in which they were all involved.

For the first month after the layoffs, each restructuring business partner had weekly touchpoint meetings with their assigned managers within the organization. Those had ended a couple weeks before, and Barbara found herself reaching out to Ivan to set up a time to touch base and discuss options to handle what was going on with Amber and her performance. Barbara and Ivan met two days later and talked about what was known – the facts of the situation. The best approach, Ivan said, was to meet with Amber to discuss her diminishing performance, as reflected on the weekly reports.

Ivan's advice was for Barbara to ask Amber what she felt was causing the decline. He explained this would help open the door for Amber to discuss what she might be feeling or experiencing that was leading to the negative impact on her performance. From there, Ivan recommended Barbara reveal more about her own prior experience and begin to relate their situations, where possible. It was important for Barbara to talk about what she did to improve her situation (and positively contribute to her prior organization) and why Barbara decided it was finally time to leave that organization. Finally, Ivan advised Barbara to work with Amber to develop a plan of action towards improvement – including whether Amber reaching out to the EAP provider was a consideration, and how regularly the two would meet to discuss progress.

Barbara met with Amber a few days later and followed Ivan's advice in what to cover and discuss with Amber. Barbara was surprised to see the relief in Amber's face, her partially relaxed shoulders, and a sigh of relief Amber let out. Amber told Barbara that she felt like there was no one to help her through everything that was happening at work, and on top of everything, she told Barbara that she had just started taking a class at the local community college a month earlier and was starting to struggle with the course workload too. Amber hadn't realized how much the stress was impacting her overall. The tension Barbara felt began to dissipate after Amber disclosed what she was going through and her openness to support. Barbara and Amber discussed some opportunities for Amber to get support (through the Employee Assistance Program's materials and use of the on-site counselor, as well as more frequent one-on-one meetings with Barbara).

Reflection Questions

1. *If Sunrise Cable did not provide restructuring business partners for managers after the layoffs, and Barbara approached you, a fellow manager, asking for ideas on what to do regarding Amber's performance, what would you recommend?*

2. *Companies often provide Employee Assistance Plans (EAPs) to employees on a regular basis. What opportunities or information does your organization's EAP include that may be beneficial to your team?*

3. *Survivor guilt exists after layoffs and in various tragedies experienced in life overall. If you were friends with Amber (and not an employee of Sunrise Cable), what advice might you give her to consider?*

"We don't develop courage by being happy every day.
We develop it by surviving difficult times and challenging adversity."
— Barbara De Angelis

Tips & Best Practices for Coping with Survivor Syndrome

1. Understand Employee Assistance Program options available for employees.

Managers should be aware of whether their organization has an EAP. These types of programs provide helpful information, typically via a website or a call-in help line, for employees related to various situations, such as finances/budgeting, stress management, helping a sick relative, deciding whether to go back to school, career services, mental illness insight, and many more. The EAP may provide a certain number of free counseling services to employees over a range of time, which can be extremely beneficial during periods of organizational change. The first step in learning more about the availability of an EAP is through an organization's Human Resources department.

2. Ensure employees know they are valued.

Managers too easily assume their employees realize they are valued in what they bring to, and do for, the organization. While that may be true, a verbal or written reminder is a great way to ensure an employee sees the message in black and white versus trying to read through any potential grey. Employees may feel more vulnerable after a change, so it is important for managers to be genuine and let them know the impact of their work.

3. Be open and available.

One of the worst reactions to layoffs that I heard during my dissertation research was of a manager who hid in his office to avoid having to interact or talk with anyone else in the organization once he learned of the news. It was the manager of a manager I interviewed, and he felt like the person did not want to be the deliverer of the bad news. Instead he chose to ride out the storm in his office until the layoffs were done. Please, DO NOT BE THAT MANAGER! Make sure you are open and available for your employees throughout the organizational change. Yes, managers are hurting too, but the employees are looking to managers for support and help in where to go or what to do because of the change occurring within the organization.

Theme #7:
Coping with the Emotional Experience

The emotions stemming from organizational change may be due to the concept of the psychological contract, or the unwritten rules between employer and employee. Elements within that contract may be intangibles such as job commitment and a quality work environment, in addition to pay, in return for work and vice versa. When a change occurs, especially one that feels unfair, the employee may see that as a breach of that contract. That feeling may lead to employee disengagement, decreased productivity, or even an employee choosing to leave the organization (even if they are not one of the employees that received a layoff notice).

Any organizational change will cause various levels of stress. As a result, individuals may feel emotions such as shock, disbelief, guilt, anger, anxiety, uncertainty, or depression. If there are pre-existing personal issues, such as the illness of a close family member, an individual's emotions may be significantly amplified. These types of emotions are normal and it is best to acknowledge them and identify healthy ways to minimize the stressors causing them.

Wayne's Story

It was 3 a.m. and Wayne was wide awake again, thinking about ways in which the organization he worked for could further reduce expenses. Wayne was a VP at Damon Manufacturing responsible for the production floor, which included several specialized machinists. The company's second largest contract was expiring at the end of the year and the client recently decided not to renew with his company, as they were not the lowest bid. Competition in the industry was getting cut throat and it was not hard to believe another much larger manufacturing company could come in at a lower price. Damon Manufacturing was now in trouble, and there were only 10 months left to figure out what was next.

With the manufacturing industry in the state it was now in, obtaining a large enough contract, or better yet, enough small to mid-sized contracts to replace the one they were about to lose was an impossible task. Wayne and his leadership team met the next afternoon to begin discussing the reality of the situation.

One thing the employees at the company did not know was that Wayne's wife, Katherine, was recently diagnosed with ovarian cancer. Wayne was one of those people who liked to keep his work and personal life separate, and this was no exception. Despite that, the emotions brought upon him by his wife's diagnosis and the upcoming loss of the large contract at Damon, made him feel like life was giving him more than he could handle. A healthy outlet he used to handle the personal and professional stress was running. Thankfully, it was something he could do anywhere, whether he had to travel, use the hospital's fitness center while his wife was undergoing treatment, or in the early morning hours in the makeshift gym he had set up in his basement with a treadmill and a weight bench. While the stress was still there, running helped him to clear his mind, if only for a short distance until the next run.

Reflection Questions

1. *What are alternatives to layoffs that organizations may consider?*

2. *Is Wayne's separation of personal and professional matters a good stance? Why or why not?*

3. *The ability of a person to maintain the level of stress that Wayne has is not sustainable for a long period of time. What or how might Wayne be able to further reduce his stress?*

"The soul always knows what to do to heal itself. The challenge is to silence the mind."
- Caroline Myss

Tips & Best Practices for Coping with the Emotional Experience

1. <u>Show vulnerability.</u>

Time and again, I hear individuals tell me of their belief that managers are not concerned with what will happen to employees who are laid off from the organization, almost to the tone of the manager being greedy and out for their own good. Yes, there are some managers I have encountered, or heard about through others, who fall into that category. The interesting thing I have learned though, is that there are significant number of managers who DO NOT fall into that category – those managers care and are concerned for employees affected by layoffs. They may not be willing to show that vulnerable side, the side I have had an opportunity to learn more about through conversations and research. Rather than weakness, vulnerability reflects openness to uncertainty and letting others see you as you, not some facade you may feel you need to put on due to a role or situation. Showing vulnerability helps employees to see you as a human, and not just "the boss."

2. <u>Find a healthy outlet for stress.</u>

In the story, Wayne had his running as an outlet and opportunity to clear his head. There are numerous healthy outlets to help in minimizing stress. It could be exercise, or watching your favorite movie, reading a book, hanging out with friends, playing with your kids at the park, or meditation. Think about those activities that would bring a smile to your face, or let you feel as though the weight upon your shoulders is not so heavy, and engage in that. It doesn't have to be for hours, but it should be something where you can find a piece of relief among all the stress you are facing.

3. <u>Minimize interaction with negative people.</u>

Misery loves company. Do whatever is possible to NOT be that company! Believe me, the more you hang around with others with a negative outlook, the more likely you are to become negative too. Somehow it always seems easier to fall into a negative mood during a difficult change, such as layoffs.

I understand that positivity and someone losing their job doesn't align, but to not get pulled into the negative swirl of conversations, gossip, and rumors you must remain somewhere in the middle.

Theme #8:
Treating Downsized Employees Humanely

Delivering life-changing news is never an easy task. Having the responsibility as a manager to tell an employee they are being laid off is no exception. Being laid off from an organization is traumatic and changes people's lives, whether for the better or for worse. Laid off employees should be treated with respect and integrity, and be provided sufficient time and space to allow them to leave the organization with dignity. It is critical that the preparation, delivery, and actions taken after the information is communicated to the employee is done so in a humane manner. Managers play a part in whether they will be the next laid off employee's story of the horror they experienced, or the compassion they felt. Laid off employees are not just a deduction to the organization's expense line, they are human beings with families, livelihoods, and feelings. Whenever possible, this should be considered.

Minh's Story

"TNT Restaurants has finally gotten *something* right," Minh thought. He was manager for the team responsible for ordering the fresh food for New York's finest restaurants located in and around Manhattan. The rumors started a few months back and employees of TNT Restaurants became a bit anxious whenever they attended a team meeting, or worse yet, a one-on-one with their manager. Earlier that week, Minh had received the nod of approval to proceed with discussing the upcoming layoffs the company would experience and how it would impact his team. With the economic downturn earlier that year, as well as the impact of the recent drought along the entire West Coast, something had to give. Minh's team was already small, so it was unimaginable their team specifically would be hit with layoffs, if that was a possibility.

Minh gathered his team first thing Thursday morning and began to discuss the changes. Due to the economic downturn, the cost of shipping had risen. In addition, the drought having an impact on the availability of many of the fresh produce items used daily in the restaurants. As a result, TNT

Restaurants was faced with a choice: pay more for less produce, or limit popular menu items. This is where Minh felt like TNT got it right. The CEO, Mike Kechnick, decided that because cutting menu items might negatively impact the customer experience, increasing produce costs would mean cuts needed to happen elsewhere in the business. It was a difficult decision to make, but one that was carefully thought through, with the impact not hitting one area more than another.

Mr. Kechnick let his management team, including Minh, know the company would need to cut two popular items from the regular menu, and offset the remaining three popular produce-heavy items by cutting headcount. This felt like the most logical decision, although it weighed heavily on Minh's heart when he heard the news. Minh gathered his team on a Thursday morning to share the news of the menu items being cut, and of the likelihood of layoffs.

Cordelia was the first to ask Minh a question after he spoke to the team, "How hard will this impact our team? Will we lose our jobs?" A great question and valid concern, Minh thought. He advised Cordelia that the company was doing everything they could to figure out how to maintain a balance between customer experience and the ability to retain employees. At this point, he was unaware if, or how many, from the team might be directly impacted. He assured his team he would make them aware of any further news as soon as he knew.

Thankfully, it was within one week that Minh was asked for insight as to who in his team should be let go. The Human Resources representative advised Minh that teams were viewing who goes and who stays based on performance. Within Minh's team, this was a challenge, as he had several great employees. If he had to identify the lowest performer by ratings, it would have to be Shana, due to an error on a large order and her two unplanned absences over the last six months. Minh felt terrible, as he knew Shana and her husband had two young children, although this was not something that he was able to take into consideration in determining who would go and who would stay.

Minh was trying to think of a way to help Shana even before he had to have the discussion with her and reveal the news. He remembered Shana had a real knack and enjoyment for photography. Over the last year, Shana had started to book engagement, high school senior, and baby pictures on the weekends. A friend of Minh's from college had his own photography business and studio, and he remembered seeing a note on his friend's Facebook page in the last couple weeks about needing a photography assistant. He decided he would reach out to him and see if the position was still open, in hopes that he could let Shana know of the opportunity when they talked.

Reflection Questions

1. *Would you have made the same decision as Mr. Kechnick? Why or why not?*

2. *If Minh has options other than to use performance to determine who goes and who stays within his team, what other factors might he consider?*

3. *What other options does TNT Restaurants have to maintain the produce expense and employees?*

"We are here to make limbo tolerable, to ferry wounded souls across the river of dread until the point where hope is dimly visible. And then stop the boat, shove them in the water and make them swim." – Ryan Bingham, *Up in the Air* (2009)

Tips & Best Practices for Treating Downsized Employees Humanely

1. <u>Do not treat downsized employees as if they are bad or tainted.</u>

In one of my prior experiences as a downsizing survivor, I remember the names of the laid off employees being communicated internally in an e-mail. It was difficult to carry on with any of them as if things were normal. Life in the organization was not normal at the time. There were employees who treated the laid off employees differently, whether by avoidance or awkwardness in their conversation. When I think about it, I'm not quite sure if including the names of the laid off employees in that communication was the right thing to do or not. In one respect, people knew who was affected without gossip or rumors; but it also felt like it put these individuals' names up in lights when all of them may not have wanted to have it so publicly known.

2. Offer career search services, if possible.

Organizations may decide to provide resources, such as career counselors, resume writing experts, networking meetings, mock interviewing opportunities, or access to internal computers and software for job searches and cover letter/resume writing. Assisting laid off employees in their next career move is the right thing to do. This shows concern and support, as it is a good faith act to help the laid off employee prepare for, and hopefully find, their next job. Providing this service to employees, whether through internal or external resources, is appreciated by employees when this type of support is provided.

3. Make clear and organized information available regarding what will happen.

Put yourself in the downsized employee's position for a few minutes and think about what those first few moments after getting the news might feel like. How well do you think your memory of all the information provided at that time might be when you are in a clearer state of mind? It is important to provide downsized employees with information in writing, typically within a packet, regarding next steps in the process, potential questions, options, etc. The information in the packet should be organized, relevant and clear. Human Resources should be available for downsized employees to ask questions after digesting the news and as they begin to review the information provided.

Appendix A:
Skills, Knowledge, and Interest Inventory

Name: _____   Date: _____

Skills
List up to 6 skills you currently have (a minimum of 3 skills should be work-related; at least 2 can be skills you have obtained outside of the organization).

_____   _____

_____   _____

_____   _____

Knowledge
List up to 5 areas of knowledge you have strengths in, whether through your current position, past positions (in this or other organizations), your studies, or volunteerism efforts. Think of this as the areas of knowledge which you might be considered close to, or as a subject-matter-expert.

_____   _____

_____   _____

_____   _____

Interests
Identify as many areas of interest you have – what would you like to learn or do? Where would you like to get more involved? These may be interests you have personally (e.g., photography, exercise) and/or professional (e.g., public speaking, grant writing, technical training).

Questions for Management's Consideration:
1. Were you aware of the skills, knowledge, and interests this employee has noted?
2. How can you better leverage this information, now that it is available?
3. What ways can you support the employee in further expanding upon these items?

Appendix B:
24 Tips to Downsize with Dignity

1. Develop a well-planned vision that is easy to understand
2. Communicate the reason the change is needed
3. Provide consistent messaging – cannot overcommunicate
4. Set the expectation that change is inevitable – it matters most how we react
5. Involve employees in the change process
6. Think about resistance to change from downsized employees, surviving employees, and other managers' perspectives
7. Build relationships with others in the organization
8. Speak the truth and align behaviors, attitudes, and words.
9. Let go. If employees are not willing to commit and want to leave, let them.
10. Be present
11. Be aware
12. Identify employees' motivators
13. Identify a strategy to "do more with less"
14. Know the skills, strengths, knowledge, and interest of employees on your team
15. Involve others in the planning and implementation of work efficiencies
16. Understand Employee Assistance Program (EAP) options available for employees
17. Ensure employees know they are valued
18. Be open and available
19. Show vulnerability
20. Find a healthy outlet for stress
21. Minimize interaction with negative people
22. Do not treat downsized employees as if they are bad or tainted
23. Offer career search services, if possible
24. Have clear and organized information available regarding what will happen

Appendix C:
Recommended Reading

Armstrong-Stassen, M. (2005). Coping with downsizing: A comparison of executive-level and middle managers. *International Journal of Stress Management, 12*(2), 117-141. doi: 10.1037/1072-5245.12.2.117

Cameron, K. S. (1994). Strategies for successful organizational downsizing. *Human Resource Management (1986-1998), 33*(2), 189-211. doi: 10.1002/hrm.3930330204

Clair, J. A., & Dufresne, R. L. (2004). Playing the grim reaper: How employees experience carrying out a downsizing, *Human Relations, 57*(12), 1597-1625. doi: 10.1177/0018726704049991

Datta, D. K., Guthrie, J. P., Basuil, D., & Pandey, A. (2010). Causes and effects of employee downsizing: A review and synthesis. *Journal of Management, 36*(1), 281-348. doi: 10.1177/0149206309346735

Gandofli, F. (2008). Cost reductions, downsizing-related layoffs, and HR practices. *SAM Advanced Management Journal (07497075),* 73(3), 52-58. Retrieved from http://search.proquest.com.library.capelle.edu/docview/231246437?accountid=279655

Gandolfi, F. (2009). Training and development in an era of downsizing. *Journal of Management Research (09725814), 9*(1), 3-14. Retrieved from http://search.proquest.com.library.capella.edu/docview/237227058?accountid=27965

Kotter, J.P. (1996). *Leading Change.* Boston, MA: Harvard Business School Press.

Lencioni, P. (2007). *The Truth About Employee Engagement: A fable about addressing the three root causes of job misery.* San Francisco, CA: Jossey-Bass.

Mirabal, N., & DeYoung, R. (2005). Downsizing as a strategic intervention. *Journal of American Academy of Business, Cambridge, 6*(1), 39-45. Retrieved from http://search.ebscohost.com/login.aspx?direct=true&db=bth&AN=156 37353&site=ehost-live&scope=site

Peters, T.J., & Waterman, R.H. (1982). *In search of excellence: Lessons from America's best run companies.* New York: Harper & Row.

Salemi, Ray. (2009). *Leading After a Layoff: Reignite Your Team's Productivity in Just 12 Weeks!* New York: McGraw-Hill Education.

Shaffer, J. (1997). Organizational communication best practices. *Strategic Communication Management, 2*(1), 16.

Shroyer, T. C. (2013). *The personal and professional experiences of downsizing managers: A qualitative exploratory study.* (Doctoral dissertation). Retrieved from ProQuest Dissertations and Theses database. (Order No. 3553381)

Sinek, S. (2011). *Start with Why: How great leaders inspire everyone to take action.* New York: Penguin Group.

Smith, F., Wright, A., & Huo, Y. P. (2008). Scapegoating only works if the herd is big: Downsizing, management turnover, and company turnaround. *Journal of International Business Strategy, 8*(3), 72-83. Retrieved from http://search.ebscohost.com/login.aspx?direct=tru&db=bth&AN=3563 7665&site=ehost-live&scope=site

About Dr. Tracy Shroyer

Tracy Shroyer, PhD, MBA is a leadership junkie, professor, project manager, and a management consultant. She has over 21 years of experience in the financial services industry.

Her primary areas of interest are leadership development, as well as organizational change, such as layoffs. Dr. Shroyer's dissertation research, published in 2013, focused on the personal and professional experiences of downsizing managers faced with decision making, implementation and managing in the aftermath.

Dr. Shroyer lives in Ohio with her husband, Tony and her smarty pants Australian Shepherds, Maverick and Emerson. You can reach Dr. Shroyer at her website www.tracyshroyerphd.com.

www.ingramcontent.com/pod-product-compliance
Lightning Source LLC
Chambersburg PA
CBHW071239220526
45468CB00002B/928